new   6⁵⁰

S0-BOG-283

IMPS · DEMONS · HOB-GOBLINS · WITCHES FAIRIES & ELVES

PANTHEON BOOKS · NEW YORK

BY LEONARD BASKIN

"The Little Gnome," a poem by Laura E. Richards,
was the source and inspiration for The Little Gnome in this book.

Copyright © 1984 by Leonard Baskin. All rights reserved under International and Pan-American Copyright Con-
ventions. Published in the United States by Pantheon Books, a division of Random House, Inc., New York, and
simultaneously in Canada by Random House of Canada Limited, Toronto. Distributed by Random House, Inc.,
New York. Manufactured in the United States of America   10   9   8   7   6   5   4   3   2   1
Library of Congress Cataloging in Publication Data. Baskin, Leonard, 1922–   Imps, demons, hobgoblins, witches,
fairies & elves. Summary: An illustrated catalogue of imps, hobgoblins, demons, and witches taken from literature
and the author's own imagination. 1. Fairies—Juvenile literature. [1. Fairies. 2. Witches] I. Title.   GR549.B37
1984   398.2'1   84-2911   ISBN 0-394-85963-4   ISBN 0-394-95963-9 (lib. bdg.)

For Helen and Jose with love

The Imp of the Perverse is
the scamp who ruins everyone's
fun, invites the rain to picnics and pa-
rades, puts holes in pails, makes faucets drip,
burns out lights, snags stockings, places the nails
that flatten tires, runs down batteries, loses keys, crosses
telephone wires, breaks pencil points, melts crayons, opens
car and house windows to the rain, tangles hair, pops buttons,
eats holes in socks, shrinks clothes, jams zippers, knots thread,
burns toast, empties gas tanks, stops elevators between floors,
loses balls, hides shoes, tangles fishing lines, makes windows
stick, delays trains, collapses umbrellas, steals kites, pops bal-
loons, spooks the cat, sinks the cake, scuttles small boats, boils
the teakettle dry, drops banana peels in your path, stains new
clothes, pops strings on violins and tennis racquets, breaks
shoelaces, snaps up window shades, dries out tubes of paint,
clogs drains, curdles milk, rusts and corrodes, makes fetid
and rancid, turns you right when you intend to go left, says
yes when you mean no, reduces and enlarges when you
wish for neither, causes you to advance when you
wish to retreat, to stop when you wish to
continue, to speak when you would
be silent and to remember what
you'd rather forget.

The Wicked Witch of the West worked her wickedness day in and day out. In the course of a single day she could frighten nearly to death four girls, six boys, two cows and any brown and white Jack Russell dog named Whiskey. And we all know of the great grief she caused Dorothy and her poor, scared dog Toto in The Wizard of Oz, *until they did her in. Fortunately for us, she has never been heard or seen since then.*

A stupid miller bragged to the King that his daughter could spin gold from straw. So the King brought the young woman into his castle and put her in a room filled with straw. He gave her a spinning wheel and left, saying, "You shall die if by morning this straw is not spun into gold." The miller's daughter wept in despair. Suddenly an odd little man appeared and asked why she was crying. After she told him, he said, "What will you give me if I spin it into gold for you?" "My necklace," she said. "Very well," said the little man as he began to spin. By morning the room was full of gold. The next day the King locked the miller's daughter in a larger room filled with more straw and uttered the same threat. This time she offered the little man her ring if he would help her. "Very well," he said, and again he spun all the straw into gold. The King was pleased, but he was also greedy and so quite a huge room was filled with straw. "Spin this into gold and you shall be my Queen." That night to the odd man's inquiry the young woman said, "I have nothing left." "Very well," he said, "then you must promise to give me your first child," to which she agreed. The next day the King found all the gold and the miller's daughter became Queen. One year later, the Queen gave birth to a child and the little man reappeared, claiming his due. To the Queen's tears and entreaties he said, "I will give you three days to discover my name, but if you cannot you must yield the child." After two long days of trying
many names to which the answer was always, "No, no, no,"
the Queen, in deep despair, sent a messenger throughout
the kingdom seeking strange and unknown names. He
reported that on a hill he saw a tiny man dancing around
a fire singing, "Tomorrow at last the child comes in,
for nobody knows I'm Rumpelstiltskin." On the
third day the little man reappeared. The Queen
asked if his name was this or that or thus,
then suddenly she said, "Is your name
Rumpelstiltskin?" "The Devil must have
told you," he shouted in a mad fury,
"for no one else knows my name."
He stamped his right foot so fero-
ciously that his leg sank deep
into the ground. Then being
entirely out of control, he
seized his left foot with
both his hands and
pulled so forcefully
that he actually
tore himself in
two and was
never seen
again.

*Jack Frost
is the writer, the artist,
the musician of winter. He
sends messages in the whitest
script, using windows and glass
doors as his writing paper. When he
snaps his fingers, everything is cov-
ered with ice. If he likes he can en-
close whole trees in clear, glassy
ice and set all the woods ring-
ing in a clashing, tinkling,
crackling song.*

In A Midsummer Night's Dream *William Shakespeare plays with love and jealousy, creating a fairyland where the tiny and beautiful Queen Titania and King Oberon make sport with their magic, confounding the towering humans. Aiding these minuscule monarchs in their regal mischief are Puck, Peaseblossom, Cobweb, Moth and Mustardseed.*

Bloody Bones
is a disgusting hob-
goblin who has lived for as
long as can be remembered in
dank, dark cupboards under stairs.
If you have such a cupboard in
your house and are brave enough
to peep through a crack, you
might see a hideous crouching
figure with blood running down
his face, his hair matted with filth
and blood, sitting on a pile of
bones and leering at you. Bloody
Bones is endlessly patient as he
crouches in the dark waiting and
watching and listening for a
chance to pounce. His hapless
victims? Naughty children who tell
lies and say bad words. Watch out!

The Tooth Fairy's teeth fall out. She plants them back in but they pop loose. She can eat only crackers and milk or mashed potatoes. She will pay for your teeth in gold.

A GREMLIN

A Gremlin is a tiny imp whose only  *purpose is to cause mischief.*

Beware the Black Dog. With its smoldering, fire-filled eyes and cavernous, gaping mouth, it haunts those dread places where the gallows once stood and lurks about waste re- gions, lonely valleys, desolate, windy hilltops and ancient ruins. It is death to touch or strike the Black Dog.

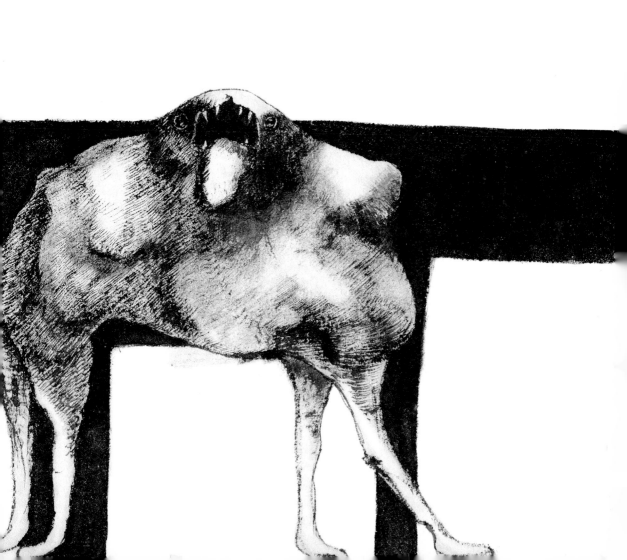

A shoemaker had become very poor and had leather enough for only one pair of shoes, which he cut out and made ready to finish the next morning. At dawn, to his astonishment, the shoes were beautifully sewn and finished. They sold directly, and with the money the cobbler bought leather for two more pairs of shoes, and prepared it for sewing. The same thing happened. With the money from the two pairs he bought leather for four pairs, and again the same thing happened, and so it went until he became wealthy. One night the shoemaker and his wife decided to watch and learn who it was that did the work. They were astounded to see two elves, completely naked, come in and finish the shoes. The wife suggested that they make gifts of clothing and shoes for the elves, which they did, and the next night they laid the clothes out on the worktable. The elves donned their new finery, danced on the table and sang:

Now we're boys so fine and neat,
Why cobble more for others' feet?

and disappeared. And although they never came again, the shoemaker remained wealthy and lucky his whole life.

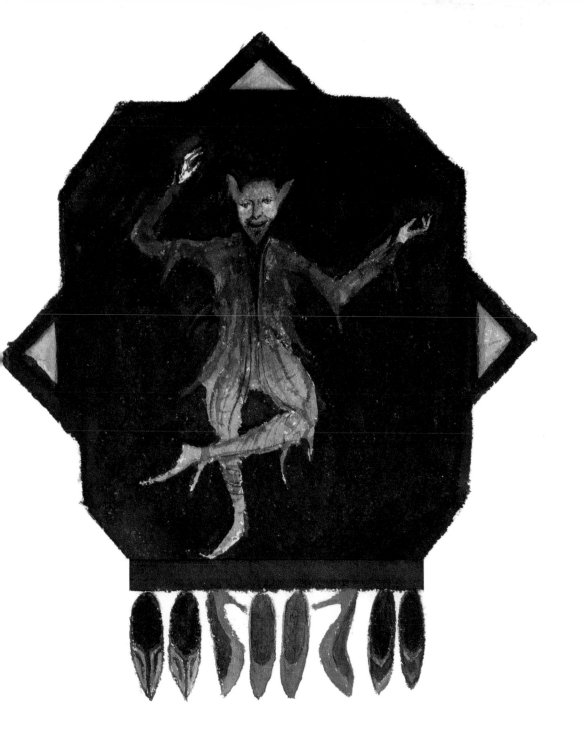

Cormoran, Blunderbore, Thunder-bell, Gargantua...these are the terrible giants that Jack killed, though he was as small as Tom Thumb. Jack was so clever at killing giants that he became known as Jack the Giant Killer and was made a knight of King Arthur's Round Table. After he sought out and destroyed the vicious giants who terrorized the people of the realm, he sent their terrible heads to King Arthur.

The Little Gnome was very happy but his wife was terribly sad; he tried to amuse her, did tricks with a pig, a parrot and a monkey–to no avail. He left home seeking various beings to amuse his wife– a blinking bear, an octopus waltzing with a whale, a Pattyfool with eyes in its tail, a linking loon who plays the bassoon, and other even odder and funnier creatures–but to no avail. The Little Gnome's wife was not amused; she continued crying and remained profoundly unhappy. In despair, the Little Gnome tore his purple hair and became sorrowful, for he'd had enough of laughing all alone. "I too," he said, "will cry." As the tears flowed away like a rivulet at play, his melancholy wife seeing his sadness cried,

> "Haw, haw.
> Here at last is something
> funny you have found, found, found."
> She laughed, "Ho! Ho! He! He!"
> And she chuckled with loud glee.
> And she wiped away her little husband's tears, tears, tears.
> And since then, through wind and weather,
> They have said "He! He!" together,
> For several hundred thousand merry years, years, years.

*I wait at windy corners with
my birds. If you blink I am
not there–but my birds circle
over the spot. They will lead you
to me. See my eyes? They tell
you to follow me, but they do not
urge you to trust me–I am the
Witch of Dark Adventures.*

This small, nervous, immensely en-
ergetic demon must through complex
interconnections be related to a recent visi-
tor from extraterrestrial space. This super-ac-
tive Demon of Energy terrifies the fat, the slug-
gish, the slow, the lazy, the lackadaisical, the torpid
and lackluster. The demon's aim is to galvanize these
shameful sloths into fat-falling-away motions. He is thus
their friend, helping them to lesser weight, better health and
usefulness. But the Demon of Energy does considerably more
than that. In a voice too shrill to be heard by human ears, it sets
dogs to howling and running after cats. It keeps the birds in a
twitter on spring mornings and the crickets chirping all night; it
stirs the air at parties, whips crowds into feverish excitement
and in some houses doesn't give the dust a chance to settle. The
demon is also a motivator of artists, stoking their fires, fanning
the flames of their genius and prodding them to achieve-
ment, production and fulfillment. The demon sits in-
visible but parrotlike on the shoulder of the pro-
ductive composer and painter, exhorting them
to a frenzy of work. It energizes us all; we
thrive on its exertions. Without the Demon of Energy we might all be sloths.

Tinkerbell was a very tiny fairy. She was not very nice. She was jealous and tried to harm Wendy.

TINKERBELL

The three Billy Goats Gruff wanted to eat the delicious-looking grass growing across the brook. To get there they had to cross a bridge guarded by a terrible, ugly troll. When the troll heard the first and littlest Billy Goat Gruff trip-trap, trip-trap across the old wooden bridge, he roared, "Who's that trip-trapping over my bridge?" "Only I, the littlest Billy Goat Gruff," came the answer. "I'll gobble you up," said the troll. "Oh, don't take me. I'm too little, but my bigger and fatter brother is coming." And the troll let the littlest Billy Goat Gruff cross the bridge. Next came the middle Billy Goat Gruff, and the same thing happened to him. Finally, the big Billy Goat Gruff came crashing across the bridge, and the terrible troll said he would gobble him up. "Well then," said the biggest Billy Goat Gruff, "come gobble me!" And when the troll came up onto the bridge he was sent to kingdom come by the mighty horns of the biggest Billy Goat Gruff. And the three Billy Goats Gruff grew very fat on the far and greener side of the brook.

THE TROLL IN ''THREE BILLY GOATS GRUFF''

In Shakespeare's The Tempest, *Lord Prospero, who has been betrayed into exile by a false brother, sets up a kingdom of his own on a desolate island inhabited by the mythical creatures Ariel and Caliban. Ariel, the spirit of airy sight, is made to work magic for Prospero, and Caliban, the son of a blue-eyed hag, toils as his slave. Both are unwilling servants and seek their freedom from Prospero—Ariel through kindness, and Caliban through deceit.*

The
Sly Devil
has many odd
names: Beelzebub, As-
modeus, Apollyon, Satan,
Lucifer and Mephistopheles. He
is the prince of the underworld,
but he wanders the earth tempt-
ing humans. A wonderful and
ancient story tells of Dr. Faust
selling his soul to Mephistopheles in return for the promise of
a lifetime of youthfulness and
ceaseless pleasure–which lasts
until the Devil finally reappears
to collect the old debt.
The day of reckoning
is always terrible
and teaches us
not to be
tempt-
ed.

Sometimes there are
people who feel that
nobody cares about
them. They want
people to love them
but nobody does. On
the outside they look
ugly and witchlike.
They are witches, but
they are good, and
you never know it.
They make you see
your watch when
you have lost it. They
put another cookie in
the bag when you thought
it was empty. They
get you home safely
on dark nights and
do other good deeds.
But no one knows of these
good things. No one loves
them, and they are
very, very sad.

THE WITCH OF SECRET GOOD DEEDS

Peo-
ple make
the mistake of
leaving Jack-o'-Lan-
terns outside, ignored and
untended, after Halloween. They
don't like such neglect. So the mo-
ment the sun sets they come to the
windows. They glow as though their
candle were still aflare. They want
you! Don't pull down your hat.
And don't hide under the blanket
or behind the door. Jack-o'-Lanterns
are very sly; they know every trick.
Only one thing satisfies them: hear-
ing you scream. Or knowing you
love them and will go with them
and make someone else scream.

The Guardian Angel is filled with strength and glows with golden goodness. As it carries your hopes on its golden wings, it will win against all the creatures of the dark and leave a golden trail of peace behind its flight.

Respecting the sensitivity of members
of the population to which this book is
dedicated, I wish to acknowledge that
the characters I have chosen to picture
are but a random and tiny sampling.
I say *adieu* to the Banshee, Barguest,
Bogey-Beast, Boggart, Boggle-Boo,
Bogie, Booback, Booman, Brag-Buggan,
Bug-a-Boo, Bugs, Bullbeggar, Capelth-
waite, Cauld Lad of Hilton, Cearb,
Clap-Cans, Colt-Pixie, Derricks, Dob-
by, Dobie, Dunnie, Dunter, Fane, Frid,
Galley-Beggar, Galley-Trot, Grogan,
Hagge, Henkie, Hobmen, Jack-in-Irons,
Klippe, Knockers, Licke, Lob, Lubbard-
Fiend, Lull, Manx Buggane, Mara, Melsh
Dick, Mumpoker, Orph, Padfoot, Peg
Powler, Phouka, Picktree Brag, Pinch,
Pixie, Pokey-Hokey, Puck, Puddlefoot,
Rawhead, Redcap, Redshank, Sib,
Skillywidden, Skrike, Spunkie, Tan-
kerabogus, Tatterfoal, Tom-Poker, Trow,
Urisk, Wight & Yarthkins. *Adieu, adieu*.

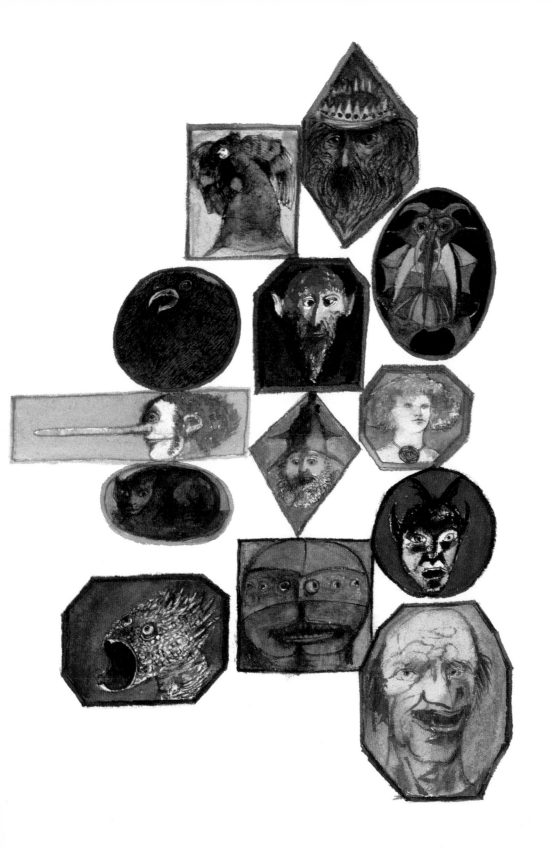

1186 QZVT